LEFT HAND MUFFLES

Muffles are a standard part of pedal harp technique. However, many lever harp players are not familiar with them. This is not surprising, since the bass strings are generally the ones that need muffling, and pedal harps have many more bass strings than lever harps. But if your lever harp has more than about an octave below middle C, muffling is a technique that will make your playing cleaner and more melodious. Which muffles to use, and where to use them, are dictated by personal preference. The muffles I have indicated in this music are suggestions only. The resonance of your harp, particularly in the bass, and your ear will tell you whether a muffle is needed. Playing these pieces on various lever harps, I have found that some harps require lots of muffling, and some can be played with very few muffles, due to their shorter bass ring.

Many of the muffles utilize a flat hand position. Imagine that you are going to push open a swinging door with your left hand. Try it. What does your hand look like? You place your palm flat against the door with your thumb and fingers pointing towards the ceiling. This is pretty much what you will do when playing in a flat hand position. Now let's try it on your harp.

Exercise #1.
Place your left hand flat against the strings with your thumb on middle C pointing straight up. Your 4 fingers won't be pointing straight up, they'll be at a slight angle where they are comfortable. Your palm and the full length of all your fingers should be in contact with the string. No gaps are allowed. The bottom part of your hand below your thumb will probably be covering a few strings above middle C. Practice placing your hand like this several times until you can place the entire length of your hand and fingers at the same time. Now let's see how this works to muffle the strings. With your right hand, play some of the strings in that octave below middle C, and then use your left flat hand muffle. Do you hear how the strings are stopped? (Some strings lower on your harp may still be ringing sympathetically.) If some of the strings in the octave that you were trying to muffle still are sounding, your hand isn't FLAT against the strings. If you get buzzes when you muffle, then you're not placing your hand on the strings with enough conviction! If you wander into the strings, you'll get buzzes. If you place your hand firmly, with all parts of your hand and fingers at the same time, you won't buzz. Practice muffling in this manner until all of the strings stop at the same time.

Exercise #2.
Now that you have ma[...] we'll pluck some strin[...] Here's a visualization trick that I learned from a wonderful harp teacher, Suzanne Balderston. Look at the big knuckles of your left hand, the ones where your fingers attach to your hand. Imagine that these knuckles are a drawbridge. You're going to raise these knuckles (the drawbridge) while you play. Here's how it works. Start with your flat hand position, with your thumb on middle C (as we did above). As you pluck your thumb, raise the drawbridge. The tips of your 4 fingers should stay on the strings, and the rest of your hand is drawn away from the strings (leading with the drawbridge knuckles). If you don't lift your hand from the strings, you'll get a harmonic (which we don't want here) instead of a nice clear note played with your thumb. Practice this, placing your hand flat and then playing your thumb, until it feels comfortable.

Exercise #3: Flat thumb.
In "real life", you actually want to play the thumb AT THE SAME TIME as you muffle the strings (instead of afterwards). It should be one continuous motion. This way, the note played by the thumb will cover up any noises made by the muffling, and the tone will not be interrupted. So your next exercise is to place your hand flat against the strings (as above) and play the thumb at exactly the same time that your hand contacts the strings. Practice this until it is comfortable. In this music, the notation for this is a + sign, instead of a fingering. The + means to muffle with a flat left hand and play the note with your left thumb at the same time.

Exercise #4: Flat 4.
Sometimes you want to play one note and muffle the strings above it at the same time. For this, you'll play with a flat 4th finger. It is the same principle as Exercises #2 and #3, except that you will pluck with the 4th finger instead of the thumb. In this music, this is notated with a + as well as a "4."

Exercise #5: Low register muffle.
When you want to muffle the lower register of the harp, just place your hand flat against the strings you want to muffle, as in Exercise #1. This is the notation for a bass register muffle. You decide which strings to muffle, depending on the music and the range of your harp.

You can read and print explanations of more muffling techniques at
www.harpcenter.com/muffles

Stairway to Heaven
(Intermediate Harp Version)

Lever harp players:
Set low F#, low G#, middle F# and high F#.

Words and music by
Jimmy Page and Robert Plant
harp arrangement by Sylvia Woods

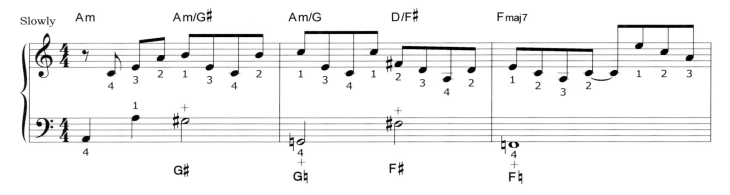

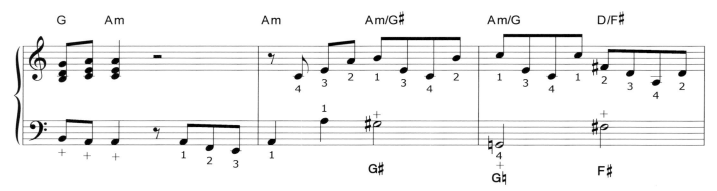

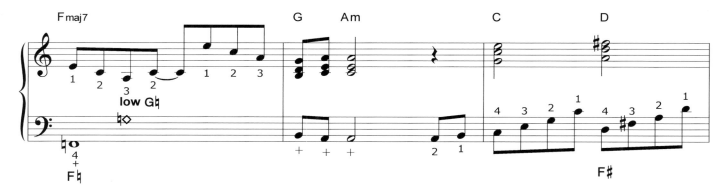

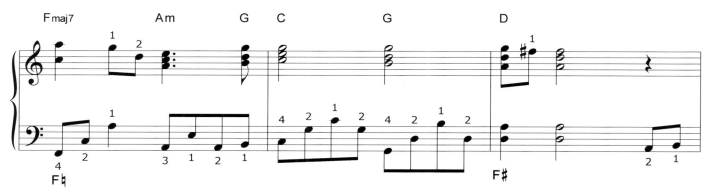

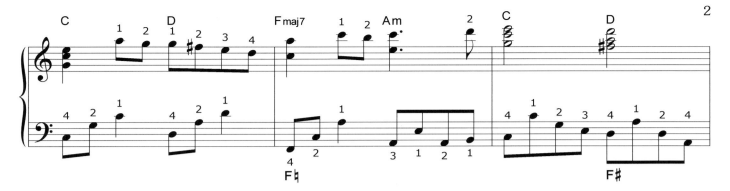

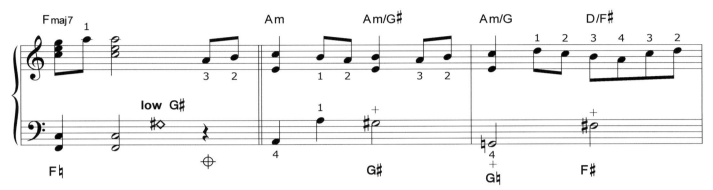

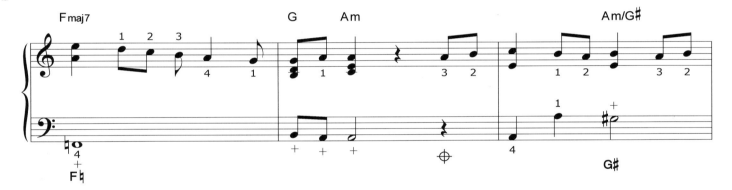

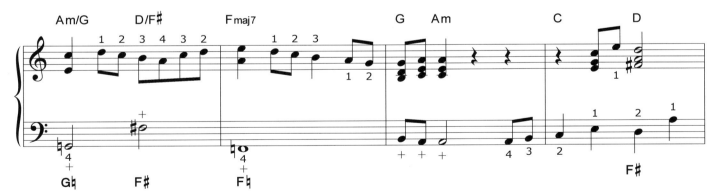

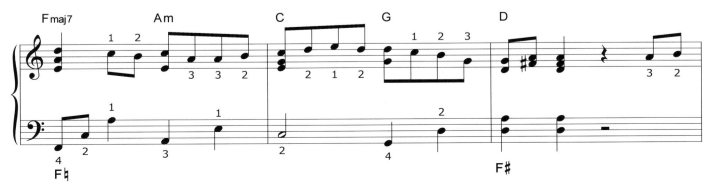

3

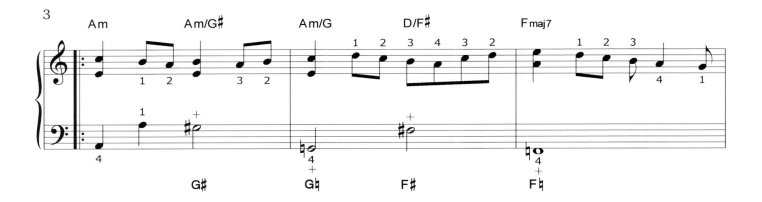

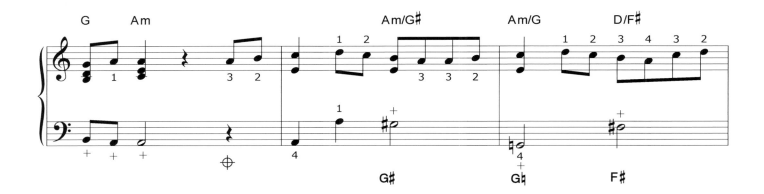

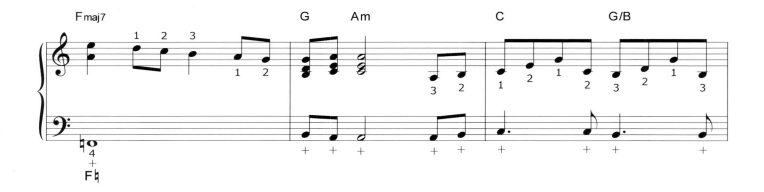

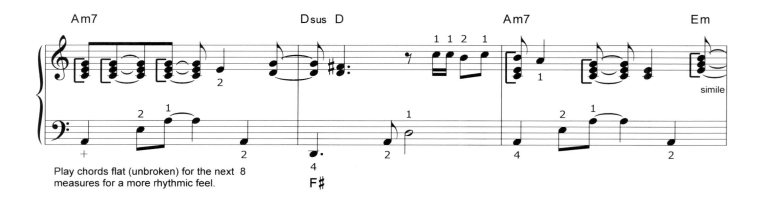

Play chords flat (unbroken) for the next 8 measures for a more rhythmic feel.

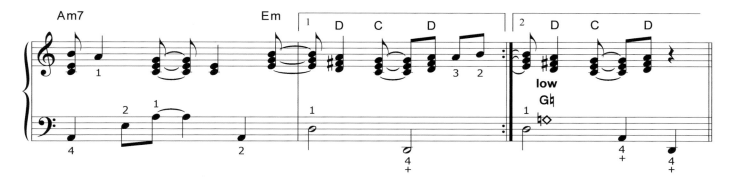

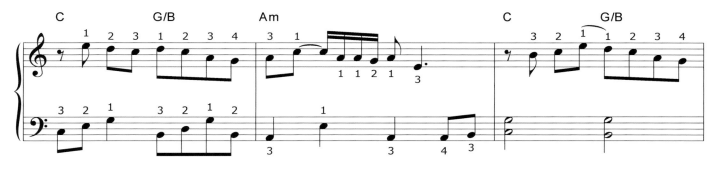

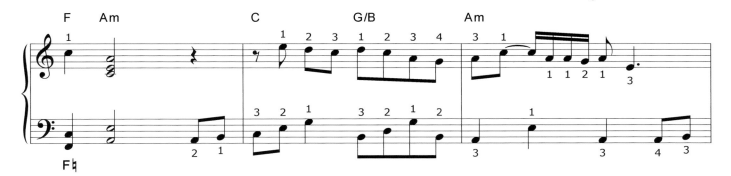

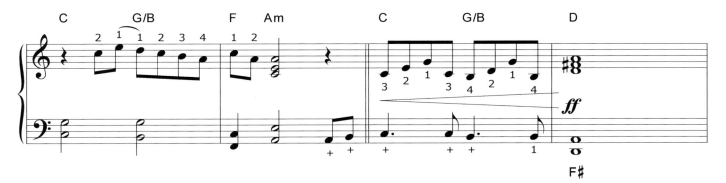

5

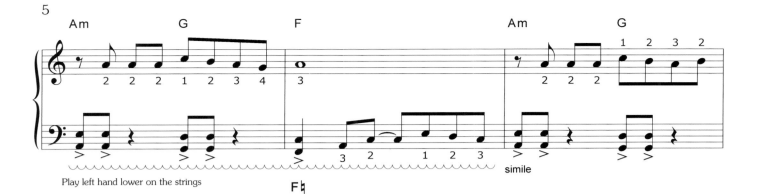

Play left hand lower on the strings

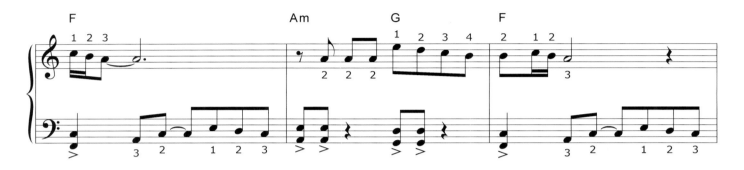

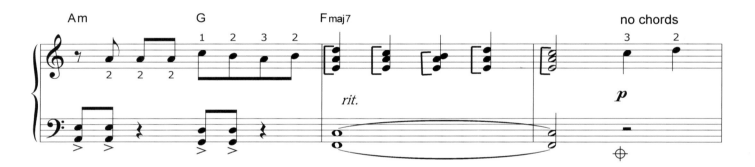

Pedal Harp Bass Line
Pedal harpists may substitute this bass line in the first 4 measures, and whenever this bass pattern repeats throughout the piece.

Stairway to Heaven
(Easy Harp Version)

Lever harp players:
Set F# and G# below middle C,
  and the F# above middle C.

On 26-string harps, play both hands 1 octave higher.

Words and Music by
Jimmy Page and Robert Plant
harp arrangement by Sylvia Woods

7

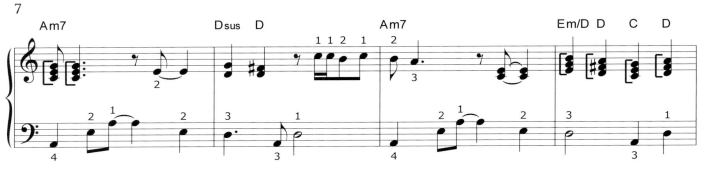

Play chords flat (unbroken) for the next 8
measures for a more rhythmic feel.

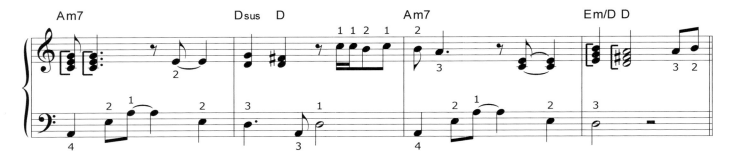

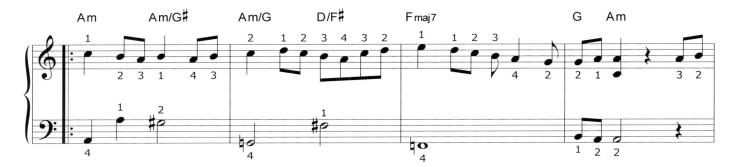

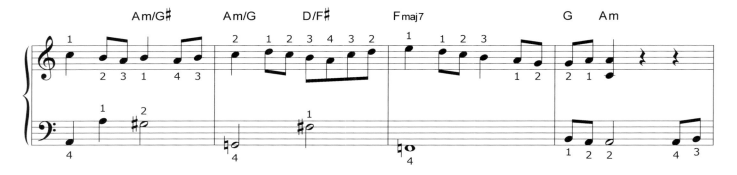

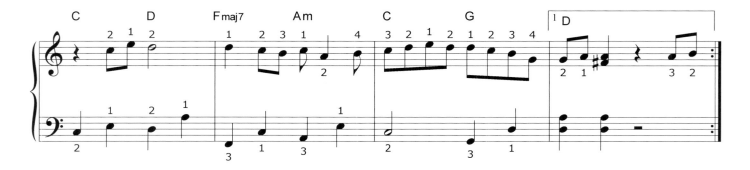